Kenneth J. Kogut, Ph.D., P.E.

WORDS TO LIVE BY

(A Not All Inclusive Look at Life in Words)

outskirts
press

Words to Live By
(A Not All Inclusive Look at Life in Words)
All Rights Reserved.
Copyright © 2019 Kenneth J. Kogut, Ph.D., P.E.
v4.0

Outskirts Press, Inc.
http://www.outskirtspress.com

ISBN: 978-1-9772-1012-8

PRINTED IN THE UNITED STATES OF AMERICA

Dedication

To my wife and best friend, Darlene, who has believed in me
and stood by my side through life's walk.

Table of Contents

On Life   1
On Travel   9
On Sports   12
On Cuisine Dining and Food   15
On Animals   18
On Finances   21
On Personal Care   24
On Education   27
On Politics   30
On Toasts   33

PREFACE

IN LIFE, ONE has the unique opportunity to travel with time, and take the time, to experience…experience. I have always enjoyed how a play on words can produce some interesting, and, for the most part, an enjoyable look at the use of the English language.

In today's society, it seems that the rush to have the biggest house, the fanciest car, and the most money, has left many individuals in the awkward position of not really knowing the real reality about reality. I hope that one finds enjoyment within this collection of phrases, sayings, and thoughts. Some may be familiar, and others are an expression of observations among various subject matters. The collection, I hope, will allow some individuals to take a second, to take a second look at life as seen through some notable notables', along with yours truly.

Please enjoy a momentous enjoyable thought, and reflect upon an unreflected second thought, in what has become our world of words, today.

ON LIFE

ON LIFE

Philosophy of Life: If you are not here, you have to be somewhere else.
Corollary: Everyone has to be somewhere at some time. That's Life!

Ken Kogut (KJK)

Is the glass half full or half empty?

Anonymous

"To Live, to err, to fall, to triumph, to recreate life out of life…."

James Joyce

Life is a piece of cake. It all depends on how you slice it.

KJK

If I have learned one thing in life, its believing in yourself IS the most
important thing

KJK

Help to some people is sometimes hindrance to others

KJK

Do it now. Don't live in the future. Thus, what if?

KJK

Life sometimes feels as though you are traveling the wrong way down a one way street.

KJK

If one needs space, how much is enough?

KJK

When people say have a "nice day", then the pressure is on you. Just wish, Day, afternoon, evening. I don't want the pressure of having a "nice" day….

George Carlin

What truly is the difference between "itsy bitsy, and teeny weeny", on pizza slices.

Ed Norton – The Honeymooners

If one does not drink beer, does that mean they are hopless

KJK

If one buts butts, then is it truly cheek to cheek.

KJK

Believe in something for another world, but don't be too set on what it is, and then you won't start out that life with a disappointment. Live your life so that when you loose, you are ahead.

Will Rogers

When one decides to buy something with all the bells and whistles, what does one get, more bells or more whistles?

Darlene Kogut (DAK)

Can I have your name, I'll give it back to you in a little while.

Groucho Marx

He'll regret it to his dying day, if ever he lives that long.

From the Movie – The Quiet Man

I thought I thought a thought; but when I thought about the thought, the thought wasn't worth thinking about.

KJK

I tried to time a New York minute once, but it went by too fast.

KJK

In life, one learns to value your friendships, and tolerate your acquaintances. Unfortunately, people have not learned to discern the difference.

KJK

I wouldn't belong to any country club that would have me.

Groucho Marx

Things may come to those who wait, but only the things left by those who hustle.

Abraham Lincoln

Age is a question of mind over matter. If you don't mind, it doesn't matter.

Satchel Paige

If they don't love you with onion on your breath, they shouldn't love you at all.

Jeff Smith

You can lead a horse to water, but a pencil must be lead.

Stan Laurel

You are who you are, and if you aren't, you're not you.

Sparky Anderson – Former Detroit Tigers Mgr.

Wherever you go, there you are.

Professor Irwin Corey

Wine, in moderation makes a happier life, a more gentle life… and you live longer too.

Robert Mondovi

If one installs a phone in the bathroom or a boat, is it truly considered a "head" phone.

Darlene Kogut (DAK)

I reflected upon my father's death, at the wake, and there are times when one does not want the best seats in the house.

KJK

In the meal of life, there are no free lunches, but there are discounted dinners….only smaller portions.

KJK

Wisdom is knowing what to do next. Skill is knowing how to do it. Virtue is doing it.

Thomas Jefferson

What do you call two boat slips together…. A pair-of-docks (a paradox)

KJK

When you come to a fork in the road – take it!

Yogi Berra

If you have a problem thinking ahead, then think an arm.

KJK

Life is centered around responsibilities and commitments. You are responsible for commitments and you are committed to your responsibilities.

KJK

Does ordering a half a pear mean one?

KJK

What time span does one place on the statement "a slice of life"?

KJK

The problem with closet comedians is that they cannot get past the hanging trousers. The corollary, no one opened up the door.

KJK

I went to the dentist and he wanted to put in a "permanent temporary" tooth. My question is, for how long – a little while or forever?

KJK

NORGE (Norway). Refrigerators, and the next thing you know – they are a country.

KJK

Some people have an idea that you cannot be in business and lead an upright life, whereas the truth is that no one succeeds in business to any great extent, who misleads or misrepresents.

KJK

Your hometown is not where you're from. It's who you are.

Arnold Palmer
50th Latrobe H.S. Reunion

What is the difference between a hang-over or a hang-under – One more drink over the limit of which you thought one more over your previous limit was the limit.

KJK

A restaurant posted a sign "Proper dress required". I guess gentlemen are excluded from dining there --- No coat and tie is acceptable – let alone you need to wear the "Proper dress".

KJK

There is no limit to the ingenuity of more if it is properly applied under conditions of peace and justice.

Winston Churchill
Nobel Prize Literature – 1953

If one adventures confidently in the direction of his dreams, and endeavors to live the life which he has imagined, he will meet with a success unexpected in common hours.

Henry David Thoreau

Far better it is to dare mighty things, to win glorious triumphs, even though checkered by failure, then to take rank with those poor spirits who neither enjoy much nor suffer much, because they live in the gray thoughts that knows not victory over defeat.

Theodore Roosevelt

If you are ever thwarted, remember, "Four thwarts make a gallon".

KJK

You will continue to suffer if you have an emotional reaction to everything that is said to you. True power is sitting back and observing things with logic. If words control you that means that everyone else can control you. Breathe and allow things to pass.

Warren Buffett

When you come to a roadblock, take a detour.

Barbara Bush - Former First lady

Be bold in your caring, be bold in your dreaming and above all else, always do your best.

George H. W. Bush – 41st president

Life is a mystery to be lived, not a problem to be solved.

Soren Kierkegaard

Knowing yourself is the beginning of all wisdom.

Aristotle

Life isn't about waiting for the storm to pass. It's about learning to dance in the rain.

Anonymous

ON TRAVEL

✺

ON TRAVEL

Just like downtown!

Old Chicago Saying

It just goes to show you, you can take the man out of Berwyn, but you cannot take the Berwyn out of the man.

KJK

You ("U") drive – No, you mean me drive!

Abbott and Costello
(Rental Cars)

When Darlene (Dar) and I traveled to Key West, we traveled by car from Miami, to Key Largo, to Key West. I kept saying we need to find the 'missing Key"…..the Garage Key. We were traveling with very good friends. Then…we found it! An island off the Seven Mile Bridge with a broken bridge to the island. The missing Key…The Garage Key.

KJK

So the American gymnast asked the Russian gymnast, Are you Russian? – and the "Russian" responded, No, just kind of taking it easy (A thought during the '94 Summer Olympics).

KJK

So the classical musician asked the person waiting at the bus stop, what do you think of Debussy? The person answered and said…I take it every morning to work.

KJK

We're off to see the sea, to see what we can see.

The Three Stooges

Not until we are lost, do we begin to understand ourselves.

Henry David Thoreau

The journey, not the arrival matters.

T.S. Eliot

Two roads diverged in a wood and I – I took the one less traveled by, and that has made all the difference.

Robert Frost

I love to travel, but hate to arrive.

Albert Einstein

Do not follow where the path may lead. Go instead where there is no path and leave a trail.

Ralph Waldo Emerson

The world is a book, and those who do not travel read only one page.

Saint Augustine

ON SPORTS

ON SPORTS

Who's on First Routine. (Q: Which field position is left out of the routine…only one…Right Field)

Abbott and Costello

Ju (you) will ski…Ju will not ski.

Buddy Hackett
(German accent)

How would you like to go sailing over the clubhouse, Alice.

Ralph Kramden - The Honeymooners

Addressing a golf ball…Hello Ball.

Ed Norton - The Honeymooners

When dealing with hockey players, one must wonder, Do they really puck around?

KJK

It's not over, 'til it's over.

Yogi Berra

You get up, brush your teeth, and go play football.

Mike Ditka
'91 playoffs

When things get tough, you bend over spit, and the ideas come.

Tom Madden
(On Football)

A perfect round of golf: The true object of the perfect round of golf, is never pull your putter out of your bag during a round of golf.

KJK

If you watch a game, it's fun. If you play it, it's recreation. If you work at it, it is golf.

Bob Hope

The most rewarding things you do in life are often the ones that look like they cannot be done.

Arnold Palmer

I'll have a Mr. Palmer. (How Palmer ordered an Arnold Palmer drink, followed by a wink)

Arnold Palmer

If you ever teed up your golf ball and hit it into the water with your tee shot, Dad always said, make sure you wash your ball first before you tee it up. Great advice!

Joseph Kogut (Dad)

I play golf with friends sometimes, but there are never friendly games.

Ben Hogan

ON CUISINE DINING AND FOOD

On Cuisine, Dining, and Food

In regards to restaurants, I have reservations about reservations.

KJK

If there is anything I like more than honey and ketchup, its bologna and whip cream, and we don't have any.

Moe
The Three Stooges

Want some dip, dip?

KJK

We were hungry when we got to Moscow, So-ve-et (So we ate…play on words…Soviet)

Groucho Marx

Sometimes when we order a la carte, we find that we get more a la, than carte

KJK

What is an orange orange?

KJK

I would like to introduce you to the Nut Family…Wal, Pea, and Hazel.

Anonymous

I went up to the candy counter and asked if they have any pareils. They responded and said, no, we only have nonpareils (play on words).

KJK

What is a non – nonpareil…. a pareil? A candy play on words, and one that may not exist.

KJK

Life is uncertain. Eat dessert first

Ernestine Ulmer

I cook with wine. Sometimes I even add it to the food.

W.C. Fields

The secret of success in life is to eat what you like and let the food fight it out inside.

Mark Twain

Everything you see I owe to spaghetti.

Sophia Loren

If you eat bacon, are you considered baconized?

KJK

After a good dinner one can forgive anybody, even one's own relatives.

Oscar Wilde

ON ANIMALS

On Animals

Has the deer a little doe? Yea, two bucks.

Larry
The Three Stooges

Do you know of a deer dear?

KJK

The oily bird catches the worm. (Twist on oil wells)

Curly
The Three Stooges

If one sees a bear with no hair, is that truly a bare bear?

KJK

Dogs have owners, cats have staff.

Anonymous

Thousands of years ago, cats were worshiped as gods. Cats have never forgotten this.

Anonymous

A Horse! A Horse! My kingdom for a horse!

Shakespeare

Of all the animals, man is the only one that lies.

Mark Twain

"Meow" means "woof" in cat.

George Carlin

ON FINANCES

ON FINANCES

Easel come, easel go.

Curly
The Three Stooges
(The subject of money)

Money is not the most important thing in the world. Love is. Fortunately, I love money.

Jackie Mason

A bank is a place that will lend you money if you can prove that you don't need it.

Bob Hope

Anyone who lives within their means suffers from a lack of imagination.

Oscar Wilde

Money often costs too much.

Ralph Waldo Emerson

Car sickness is the feeling you get when the monthly payment is due.

Anonymous

Always borrow money from a pessimist, he doesn't expect to be paid back.

Anonymous

It frees you from doing things you dislike. Since I dislike doing nearly everything, money is handy.

Groucho Marx

If inflation continues to soar, you're going to have to work like a dog just to live like one.

George Gobel

If all the economists were laid end to end, they'd never reach a conclusion.

George Bernard Shaw

Someone stole all my credit cards, but I won't be reporting it. The thief spends less than my wife did.

Henny Youngman

What is the difference between a taxidermist and a tax collector? The taxidermist takes your skin.

Mark Twain

ON PERSONAL CARE

ON PERSONAL CARE

What color should I dye my hair? Green, orange, brown…Henna color at all.

Shemp
The Three Stooges

How long have you had a weak back? Oh, about a week back.

Larry
The Three Stooges

Oh, Oh, Oh, Oh, I just had four kinks (Kings) in my back (A play on cards)

Larry
The Three Stooges

When an ear was taken off with a sword in pirate times, How much did they charge…A buck an ear (buccaneer).

KJK

Those are my principles, and if you don't like them….well I have others.

Groucho Marx

Families are like fudge... mostly sweet with a few nuts.

Anonymous

Some cause happiness wherever they go; others whenever they go.

Oscar Wilde

I find television very educational. Every time someone turns it on, I go in the other room and read a book.

Groucho Marx

ON EDUCATION

ON EDUCATION

Seven years of college, right down the drain

John Belushi
Animal House

If one plays on words, is that person considered a verbal musician.

KJK

Education of our youth is paramount to our future.

KJK

Education is what remains after one has forgotten what one has learned in school.

Albert Einstein

The roots of education are bitter, but the fruit is sweet.

Aristotle

An investment in knowledge pays the best interest.

Benjamin Franklin

Action is the fundamental key to success.

Pablo Picasso

Keep away from people who try to belittle your ambitions. Small people always do that, but the really great make you feel that you, too, can become great.

Mark Twain

Do not train children to learning by force and harshness, but direct them to it by what amuses their minds, so that you may be better able to discover with accuracy the peculiar bent of the genius of each.

Plato

Tell me and I forget. Teach me and I remember. Involve me and I learn.

Benjamin Franklin

You can't direct the wind but you can adjust the sails.

Anonymous

ON POLITICS

On Politics

If not you, then who? If not now, then when?

Bobby Kennedy
(Regarding John F. Kennedy, running for President)

We shape our buildings, and after that, the buildings shape us.

Winston Churchill

Loyalty to country ALWAYS. Loyalty to government, when it deserves it.

Mark Twain

Politics is for the present, but an equation is for eternity.

Albert Einstein

You may fool all of the people some of the time, you can even fool some of the people all of the time, but you cannot fool all of the people all of the time.

Abraham Lincoln

Politics is supposed to be the second-oldest profession. I have come to realize that it bears a very close resemblance to the first.

Ronald Reagan

There are always too many Democratic congressmen, too many Republican congressmen, and never enough U.S. congressmen.

Anonymous

Why pay money to have your family tree traced; go into politics and your opponents will do it for you.

Anonymous

All people are born alike — except Republicans and Democrats.

Groucho Marx

ON TOASTS

ON TOASTS

May the worst days of your future be no worse than the best days of your past.

Anonymous

May you live to be a 100, and may the last voice you hear be mine.

Anonymous

To sight, sound, touch, to work, to laugh, and best of all, to prevail

Lauren Bacall

May friendship, like wine, improve as time advances, and may we always have old wine, old friends, and young cares.

Irish toast

Be at war with your vices, at peace with your neighbors, and let every New Year find you a better man.

Benjamin Franklin, "Poor Richard's Almanac," 1755

Too much of anything is bad, but too much Champagne is just right.

Mark Twain

To memories of our past, may they be warm in our hearts. To memories of present, may they be etched in time, to memories yet to be, may they be no less warm then our warmest memories of our past.

Old English Toast

Acknowledgements

I WOULD LIKE to sincerely thank all of the individuals who I have referenced and listed regarding a quote, phrase, or saying. Their contribution have allowed for this collection of words, to come to life, and provide an interesting look at how words can influence and allow us to reflect on a reflected moment in time, in our daily lives.

To my wife, Darlene. Thank you for being a true inspiration and guiding light in my life. Without you, this collection of words, phrases, and quotes, would have not come to fruition.

To those who have passed on, their words, in life, have been an inspiration to me, and a joy to come across and reflect upon. They have provided some interesting and light thoughts over the years in the compilation of this work. Arnold Palmer (Arnie), whom I have had the opportunity to meet over a few times, has been an inspiration to me, not only in golf, but in life. He truly conducted himself in a professional, warm, and courteous manner throughout his professional golfing, business career, and life. He was a true gentleman at heart.

I would like to lastly, but not in the least, thank Outskirts Press. They have assisted in bringing this compilation of words to life. I am truly grateful to them for selecting my manuscript for publication.

In the end, no one walks through life alone. I thank all who have made this collection of quotes, phrases, and sayings possible. Let's reflect on that.

Author

MR. KOGUT MAINTAINS a professional energy and management consulting practice serving clients in the commercial, industrial, institutional, and governmental sectors. He has been actively involved in the energy field focused on designing various energy management programs and systems, applications of energy rates, and environmental programs throughout his entire professional career. Mr. Kogut has published a number of papers on the subject of energy. He is a registered Professional Engineer (P.E.) in several states, currently holds a number of certifications in the energy field, and is an active instructor in the energy field. Mr. Kogut is also listed in several Who's Who publications, and is a recipient of a number of energy awards and honors, including induction into the Association of Energy Engineers (AEE) Energy Managers' Hall of Fame. Mr. Kogut holds a Bachelor of Mechanical Engineering (BME), a Master of Engineering (ME) degree from the University of Detroit, and holds a Ph.D. from Lacrosse University in Engineering Management. His outside interests include golf, wine, and fine dining, along with social and community endeavors. Personal interests include history related readings, along with individuals involved with contributions to science, engineering, world activities, and personal endeavors. Mr. Kogut enjoys the application of variations on words and its uses in the English language.

www.ingramcontent.com/pod-product-compliance
Lightning Source LLC
Chambersburg PA
CBHW031433250726
48656CB00002B/968